Contents

PICTURE A COUNTRY

Germany

Henry Pluckrose

W
FRANKLIN WATTS
NEW YORK • LONDON • SYDNEY

This is the German flag.

First published in 1998 by
Franklin Watts
96 Leonard Street
London
EC2A 4RH

Franklin Watts Australia
14 Mars Road
Lane Cove
NSW 2066

Copyright © Franklin Watts 1998

ISBN 0 7496 2975 4

Dewey Decimal Classification Number 914.3

A CIP catalogue record for this book is available from
the British Library

Series editor: Rachel Cooke
Series designer: Kirstie Billingham
Picture research: Juliet Duff

Printed in Great Britain

Photographic acknowledgements:

Cover: Top SOA(All Over Bild Archiv/Wilfried Gohsens),
bottom left Getty Images (Robert Everts), bottom right
Getty Images (Bob Krist).

AKG, London pp.10, 14, 25 bottom;
Getty Images pp. 8 (Oldrich Karasek), 12 (Ed Pritchard),
13 (Hideo Kurihara), 15 (Marcus Brooke), 19 (John
Wyand), 28 (Bob Krist), 29 (Robert Everts);
Robert Harding Picture Library pp. 16, 17, 18, 24, 27;
The Image Bank p.25 top;
SOA pp 9 (All Over Bild Archiv/Erik Chmil), 20 and
21 (Gudrun Petersen/Joker), 22 (All Over Bild
Archiv/Wilfried Gohsens), 23 (All Over Bild Archiv/Udo
Kroner), 26 (All Over Bild Archiv/Josef Beck);
Travel Ink p.11 (Andrew Cowin).

All other photography by Steve Shott.

Map by Julian Baker.

Where is Germany?

This is a map of Germany.
Germany is a large country
in the middle of Europe.

Here are some German
stamps and money.

German money is counted
in Deutsche Marks.

This is a view of Zugspitze, Germany's highest mountain. It is 2963 metres high and is part of the Bavarian Alps.

The German landscape

Germany has many different types of landscape. In the centre and the south, there are hills covered with forests and high mountains. In the north, the land is much flatter.

In winter, the weather is cold. Summers are usually dry and hot.

The German people

People have lived in Germany
for thousands of years. Today,
over 81 million people live in Germany.

In recent times, people from other
countries - for example Turkey and Italy -
have moved to Germany to find work.

The Porta Nigra in Trier was
built over 1800 years ago,
when this part of Germany
was in the Roman Empire.

This busy street is in Berlin in eastern Germany.

Where they live

Most German people live in cities - Bonn, Dresden, Frankfurt, Hamburg, Munich, Stuttgart.

This is Frankfurt, one of the largest cities in Germany.

Tourists like to visit Rothenburg in eastern Germany to see its old houses.

Other Germans live in smaller towns and villages.

The capital city

Berlin is the capital of Germany.
Over 3 million people live there.
Berlin is a city of wide roads,
beautiful buildings, museums
and parks.

The Charlottenburg Palace in Berlin
was built between 1695 and 1790.
It is now a museum.

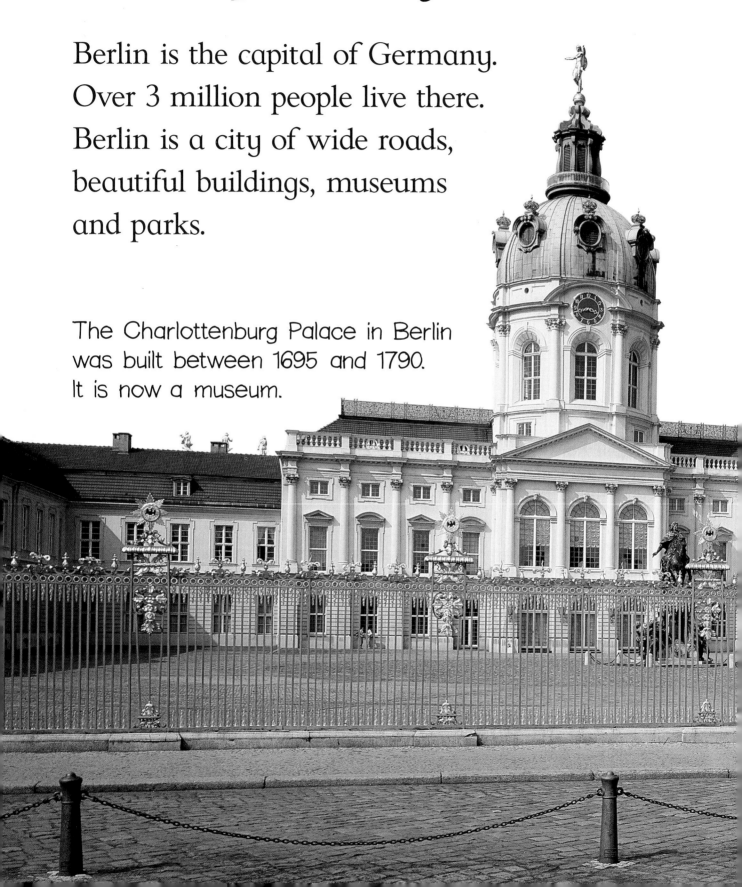

You can see Kaiser Wilhelm Church through this modern sculpture at the centre of Berlin.

Goods to sell

Germany makes and sells
many of the things we use -
from washing machines and cars
to the lenses used in telescopes.

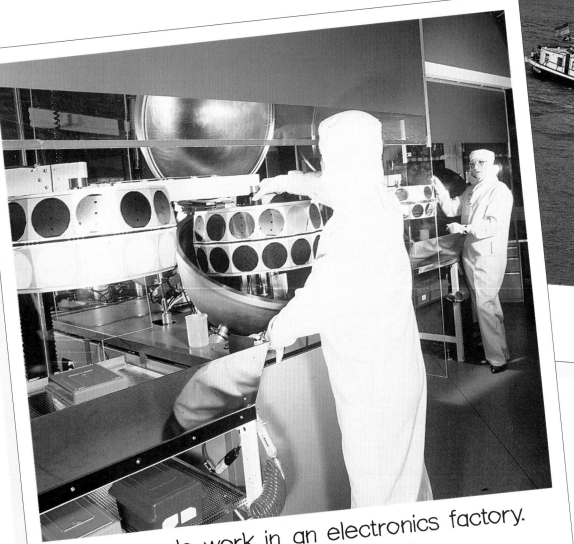

These people work in an electronics factory.
They are wearing protective clothing.

This is a barge on the Rhine as it passes through Kaub.

The River Rhine is the busiest waterway in Europe. The barges carry German goods to and from the huge port of Rotterdam in the Netherlands.

This modern German farm is in Bavaria.

Farming

German farmers grow many kinds of food - wheat for flour, hops for making beer, grapes for making wine.

This man is harvesting grapes in a vineyard above the River Mosel.

In the south, they grow fresh fruit - apples, pears and plums.

Family and home

These two pictures show
a German family at home
and out shopping together.

German children spend their time
very much like you.
They go to school, watch television,
play games and have holidays.

German food

Germans enjoy all sorts of food.
If you visit Germany, you might be offered
mince beef rolled in cabbage, spiced sausages,
bread dumplings, clear soup, salted herrings,
and cakes made of chocolate, almonds
and cream.

Out and about

Germans play many sports. German teams have been world champions in football, tennis, athletics and skating.

Water sports are popular in Germany.

Boris Becker is a German
tennis champion.

Germans also enjoy music
and going to concerts.
This statue shows Beethoven,
a famous German composer.
A composer is someone who writes music.

German festivals

There are many festivals held in
German towns and villages,
with dancing, music and plays.

Every 10 years the people
of the town of Oberammergau
act out the story of Jesus.

Every summer, crowds in Hameln watch a play about the Pied Piper of Hameln.

Visiting Germany

Many tourists visit Germany.
They go to enjoy
its beautiful countryside,
its old towns, its music festivals,
its museums and its sports.

Sigmaringen Castle in Baden-Württemberg has thousands of visitors each year.

Index

About this book

The last decade of the 20th century has been marked by an explosion in communications technology. The effect of this revolution upon the young child should not be underestimated. The television set brings a cascade of ever-changing images from around the world into the home, but the information presented is only on the screen for a few moments before the programme moves on to consider some other issue.

Instant pictures, instant information do not easily satisfy young children's emotional and intellectual needs. Young children take time to assimilate knowledge, to relate what they already know to ideas and information which are new.

The books in this series seek to provide snapshots of everyday life in countries in different parts of the world. The images have been selected to encourage the young reader to look, to question, to talk. Unlike the TV picture, each page can be studied for as long as is necessary and subsequently returned to as a point of reference. For example, a German festival might be compared with the one in their own local area; a discussion might develop about the ways in which food is prepared and eaten in a country whose culture and customs are different from their own.

The comparison of similarity and difference is the recurring theme in each of the titles in this series. People in different lands are superficially different. Where they live (the climate and terrain) obviously shapes the sort of houses that are built, but people across the world need shelter; coins may look different, but in each country people use money.

At a time when the world seems to be shrinking, it is important for children to be given the opportunity to focus upon those things which are common to all the peoples of the world. By exploring the themes touched upon in the book, children will begin to appreciate that there are strands in the everyday life of human beings which are universal.